Vienna & Bratislava Travel Guide

Attractions, Eating, Drinking, Shopping & Places To Stay

Lisa Brown

Copyright © 2014, Astute Press
All Rights Reserved.

No part of this publication may be reproduced, stored in a retrieval system, or transmitted, in any form or by any means without the prior written permission of the publisher, nor be otherwise circulated in any form of binding or cover other than that in which it is published and without similar condition being imposed on the subsequent purchaser.

If there are any errors or omissions in copyright acknowledgements the publisher will be pleased to insert the appropriate acknowledgement in any subsequent printing of this publication.

Although we have taken all reasonable care in researching this book we make no warranty about the accuracy or completeness of its content and disclaim all liability arising from its use

Table of Contents

Vienna **6**
   Culture 7
   Location & Orientation 9
   Climate & When to Visit 10

Sightseeing Highlights **12**
   Schönbrunn Palace, Garden & Zoo 12
   Ringstrasse 15
   Rathaus (City Hall) 17
   Kunsthistoriches Museum (Museum of Art History) 18
   Naturhistoriches Museum (Natural History Museum) ... 19
   Staatsoper (State Opera House) 20
   Österreichische Postsparkasse (Postal Savings Bank) ... 21
   Innere Stadt (Old Town) 21
   Stephansdom (Saint Stephen's Cathedral) 22
   The Prater 23
   Secession Building 24
   Hundertwasserhaus 25

Recommendations for the Budget Traveller **27**
   Places to Stay **28**
      Hotel Ibis Wien Messe 28
      Meininger City Hostel & Hotel Vienna 29
      Hostel Hütteldorf Vienna 30
      Hotel Hadrigan 31
      Palace Hostel Schlossherberge Vienna 32
   Places to Eat **33**
      Figls 33
      Esterházykeller 34
      Trzesniewski 34
      Tunnel 35
      Der Wiener Deewan 35
   Places to Shop **36**
      Naschmarkt 36
      Flohmarkt 36
      Leschanz Wiener Schokolade König 37
      Austrian Delights 37

Weihnachtsmarkt 37
Bratislava 39
Culture 41
Location & Orientation 43
Climate & When to Visit 45
Sightseeing Highlights 47
Bratislava Castle 47
Grassalkovich Palace 50
Michael's Gate 51
Main Square & Old Town Hall 53
Old Town Street 54
Slavin War Memorial 56
Novy Most (New Bridge) 57
St Martin's Cathedral 58
Primate's Palace 59
Slovak National Museum 60
Recommendations for a Budget Traveller 63
Places to Stay 63
Falkensteiner Hotel Bratislava 63
Hotel SET 64
Hotel Matsyak 64
Hotel Abba 65
Austria Trend Hotel 65
Places to Eat 66
UFO 66
Slovak Pub 66
Altitude Restaurant 67
Antica Toscana 67
Hradna Hviezda 68
Places to Shop 68
Old Town Christmas Market 68
Aupark Shopping Center 69
Polus City Center 69
Old Town 69
Obchodna Street 70

Vienna

Vienna is the capital of Austria and the country's epicenter for tourism, culture, business, and politics. The city was once the focal point of the Habsburg Empire and Vienna's imperial city centre is a UNESCO World Heritage site.

Visit Vienna for a step back in time, where majestic royal buildings evoke the golden ages of the Austrian Empire, where a sip of the famous Viennese Coffee transports you to a life of aristocratic luxury, and where entertaining guests has a centuries-old tradition.

Vienna is one of the most visited cities in the world and its charms overwhelm even the most reluctant tourist. World-famous museums await lovers of fine arts, exquisite little restaurants make dining a veritable event, while its vibrant atmosphere ensures that visitors can stay up until the early hours and have the time of their lives.

Culture

The city became the capital of the Austro-Hungarian Empire at the beginning of the 19th century, although its cultural significance dates back long before that. The prosperity of the past is reflected in the architectural grandeur present at every corner: here a Baroque-style royal palace, there the pleasure grounds of a princess, or the riding school of kings kept as a pride of the city for generations.

But the growth of Vienna hasn't stopped with the decline of the emperors. Today, Vienna is a meeting point for artists from all around the world, who make sure that the city never gets old or loses its edge. Concerts, festivals and events of all sorts await you on the streets of Vienna.

Often called the City of Music, Vienna boasts a surprising number of musical geniuses in its history. The Museum of Sounds, the Vienna Philharmonic, the State Opera and the innumerable annual festivals and concerts dedicated to delighting our ears, attract thousands of visitors every year. Yet don't think that by music they understand only the classical genres: techno and electronic sounds, jazz and pop/rock merge very well with the modern-day Viennese culture.

Vienna is famous for its gastronomy. Wiener Schnitzel, Viennese Coffee – the city's name is practically intertwined with food. A wide variety of potato-based dishes accompany the famous veal or beef specialties, while the selection of desserts leave your mouth watering no matter how full you may be. Which will be your favorite: the succulent, sweet Apfelstrudel, the elegant, chocolate-topped Sachertorte (served from its original cafe), or the hot peach-filled dumpling Marillenknodel? Try them all and decide for yourself.

Vienna is just as famous for its considerable wine culture as for its tasty pastry. The well-known heurigers (new wine served from the taverns next to which it grew) is a tradition which dates back to the Middle Ages. In restaurants, however, you will find mostly white wine, such as the rich, mature Chardonnay, the fruity and aromatic Riesling, or the fresh "national drink" Grüner Veltliner.

The enthusiasm for which its citizens regard Vienna is justified by the fact that it appears high on the Mercer Most Liveable Cities lists most years. This survey compares hundreds of metropolises around the globe according to their quality of living, social, political and economic status, recreational facilities, environmental conditions and many other factors. Vienna also ranks high in the list of Innovative Cities, a selection based on culture, infrastructure and markets all over the world.

Location & Orientation

Vienna is located in northeastern Austria, in the Vienna Basin, which gives the city a hilly relief of a varying altitude between 100-500 meters high. As the capital of Austria and its largest city, Vienna houses more than 25% of the population of the country, while also being the ninth largest city in Europe.

Its past is closely linked to the River Danube which once had many branches flowing majestically through the city, but at the end of the 19th century the Donaukanal was built, which redirected the mighty river. Contrary to the well-known waltz, the Danube is more gray than blue, yet standing at one of the many bridges across it, we cannot help but be impressed.

The city can be reached by most means of transportation, since it has an international airport well linked with airport shuttles, buses and trains. It is also connected to most major central European cities by train and it has good highways for cars and buses. Parking can be scarce and expensive, so consider leaving your car parked at the edge of the city, and using the public transportation during your stay.

Climate & When to Visit

Vienna has a continental climate, which means warm summers and cold winters. Although its altitude doesn't give as much freezing weather as in the western part of the country, snowfall is to be expected during the winter months up to March, just as extreme hot temperature over 30 °C during July or August. These summer months can also surprise the visitors with stormy showers during the day, but they usually don't last long.

The city provides enough entertainment to be visited all year, but the late spring, summer and early autumn months are preferred by most tourists. Dedicated to Beethoven and Schubert, the Vienna Spring Festival between March and May is a must for all those in love with Romantic music and the masters' string quartets and symphonies. The famous Vienna Festival (Wiener Festwochen) presents hundreds of performances, concerts and movies to its spectators, lasting usually from May to June.

In autumn it's time to celebrate fiction, since September hosts the Vienna Literature Festival, where leading Austrian authors present their latest work. The Viennale International Film Festival brings celebrities and independent movies as well into the city, so don't miss it if you are a passionate cinephile.

Winter is, of course, the time of Advent and Christmas. In November the streets put on their holiday decorations, pine trees and Christmas lights fill the stores and squares, and the cold winter nights are warmed with mulled wine and roasted almonds. Vienna has one of the most beautiful Christmas Markets in Europe held in many places of the city, such as the Rathausplatz (City Hall) or in front of Schönbrunn Palace. A fairytale-like site awaits the visitors of these places, with hand-made presents to buy, sweets and pastry to nibble, while carol singers prepare your heart for the miracle of Christmas.

Vienna is a wonderful place to visit at any time of the year. Each month has a special beauty to delight tourists and the city will enchant you even on a regular day. Take a trip back in time to the era of princess and emperors, or plunge into the palatal joy of the Viennese cuisine. Rediscover the thrill of love by walking hand in hand on these romantic streets with your significant other, or the excitement of the nightlife of the City of Dreams.

Sightseeing Highlights

Schönbrunn Palace, Garden & Zoo

Built in the 17th century, the Schönbrunn Palace is an imperial statement of wealth and style. Its somehow austere Baroque exterior hides a dramatic and breathtaking array of almost 1500 rooms, many of which have overwhelmingly rich decorations for today's taste. Although originally its purpose was to be a "hunting lodge", half a century later Empress Maria Theresia made it the official summer residence of the Austrian court.

To avoid seeing stars and golden angels before your eyes even after you had left, focus your attention on the truly magnificent apartments. Marvel at the sight of the Mirror Hall, where the child Mozart made his debut in front of Empress Maria Theresia in 1762, at the age of 6. Visit the Balcony Room, where the empress is depicted amidst her children by the court painter. The Marie Antoinette Room served as a dining room laid with Viennese porcelain, the court silverware, crystal glasses, and ornate with exotic orchid flower arrangements from the nursery garden, the largest collection of different kinds of orchids in Europe at that time.

The grandeur and richness of the rooms are incontestable. Flickering crystal chandeliers, golden or white stucco embellishments, allegorical frescoes of mythical gods and heroes, mirrors that seem to play optical illusions, antique furniture with vividly painted silk upholstery which could and did cost more than a fortune. This is where one of Europe's biggest ruling dynasty spent his life. Listen to the audio guide provided at the entrance, to learn little known facts about the residents, like Empress Sissy's rigorous beauty regime which allowed her to remain one of Austria's most beautiful and slender women even after four pregnancies.

The classically designed Royal Garden is a good place to go to clear your head after all that splendor. At its 1 square km wide size, there is a lot of space to just walk around, enjoying the perfectly planned and maintained natural beauty. You can try your skills of orientation at the restored Maze and rack your brain at the Labyrinth's riddles, or climb up to the Gloriette, where you can reward yourself with a cup of coffee or some cake from the cafe inside, while admiring the amazing view over the palace and the surrounding city.

A visit to the Schönbrunn Palace is definitely worth your time, and you can spend a whole day there. In this beautifully kept place you can almost see the myriad of silk and lace gowns which wrapped the countesses and noble ladies of those times, smell the perfume they left behind on their leisure walks, and listen to the hushed tones of a their elevated conversations. And who wouldn't want to imagine themselves living this luxurious life at court?

The huge grounds of Schönbrunn were big enough to cover a royal hobby or two. Emperor Franz Stephan, who was profoundly interest in natural history, founded a menagerie of exotic animals which was the base of the oldest existing Tiergarten (Zoo) in the world. This beautiful Baroque establishment functions in such a good state, that it earned the Best European Zoo award in 2010. Its inhabitants like it too, since in 2007 the first naturally conceived zoo panda baby was born. Children, who otherwise might get bored inside the palace will surely enjoy seeing the more than 500 species present at the zoo. You can also take the Panorama Train to travel from one part of the estate to the other. This mini-world offers many unmissable pleasures.

Plan ahead so you have time to see the Orangery, especially if there is a concert scheduled; the many exotic flowers and plants of the Botanic Garden, or the glass and iron structure of the Palm House with three separate climatic zones: the "cold" pavilion, the one for the temperate zone and the other for the tropical climate. For additional information, opening hours and ticket prices, visit prior to your trip the official site of the palace: http://www.schoenbrunn.at/en/

Ringstrasse

In the 19th century major cities around Europe were going through modernization and beautification. That's when Emperor Franz Joseph I ordered the building of the Ringstrasse in the place of the old city walls which were ruining the appearance of the downtown and interfered with traffic. This large circular boulevard which circles Vienna's city centre was carefully designed with each building having a particular style and appearance selected for symbolic reasons and to showcase the Empire's wealth and power.

The new Ringstrasse was such a success, that the aristocracy and affluent middle class considered it the highest honor to be able to build their own palaces among the state institutions erected by the Emperor. The distinct style of the street earned recognition and was immortalized as the Ringstrasse-style, which is characterized by reproducing and imitating various architectural styles which emerged during history.

You can take a walk on the Ringstrasse so you can admire the majestic buildings up close, or hop on to a tourist bus for a guided tour. The cheapest and best way to sightsee is by the yellow Ring tram, which goes around the boulevard every 30 minutes (with an audio-visual guide as well.)

The most important buildings of Ringstrasse are the following (from North to South):

The Votivkirche was built in a neo-Gothic style referring to the architectural style in which most impressive churches were erected at the end of the Middle Ages. The church commemorates the failed attack on Emperor Franz Joseph's life. Its airy beauty will take your breath away: the decorations on its two tall towers and the frame of the colored rose window in the middle seem to be made by lace instead of stone.

The main building of the University of Vienna, was constructed in neo-Renaissance style as a tribute to the era which uplifted the human studies and started to teach them in universities.

The Burgtheater (Court Theater) is the national theater of Austria, built in a sublime neo-Baroque style, with the statues of famous poets and playwrights on its facade.

The Parliament Building has the facade of an antique Greek temple, signifying the era in which democracy was born. In front of it stands the 15-foot tall statue of Pallas Athena, the Greek goddess of wisdom.

Rathaus (City Hall)

This institute of city administration was built in the 1870s in the neo-Gothic style of affluent cities. The bricks of which it's made are covered with natural limestone and marble plates giving it the elegant white facade. Its 97.9 meters high tower can be reached by climbing 331 steps. The tower has an iron statue of the Rathausmann, a medieval knight of the City Hall, holding a flag. An exact replica of the statue is placed in the Rathauspark right in front of the building.

The more than 1500 rooms of the building host the offices of the municipal council, regional parliament, regional government and some municipal authorities, but are often the location of other events, such as concerts and conferences too. The Festival Hall is an immense, double storey room high room decorated with numerous arcades, statues, chandeliers and rose windows. It's so big that 1,500 couples could waltz across it at the same time – so it's the perfect place for the annually held Life Ball.

The Rathaus presents a beautiful backdrop to the Christmas Market which takes place every year in front of it with carol singers lighting the mood, local merchants selling delicate handcrafted gifts and freshly made food and beverages keeping the visitors warm.

Kunsthistoriches Museum (Museum of Art History)

A few meters away from the Ringstrasse lies the Maria-Theresien-Platz (Maria Theresia Square) with two buildings that face each other: the Museum of Art History and the Natural History Museum. They were both created by the same architects around the same time at the end of the 19th century to host and make public the remarkable art collection of the Habsburg dynasty.

The Kunsthistoriches Museum's picture gallery boasts the paintings of well-known Flemish masters such as van Eyck, Albrecht Dürer, Arcimboldo, Rembrandt and and Vermeer, and a number of world-famous Italian paintings as featured well: Tintoretto's Susanna and the Elders, Raphael's Madonna of the Meadow, Caravaggio's The Crowning with Thorns and so on. It also has the largest collection of Brueghel the Elder, which has an immense intellectual and material value by itself.

Although the history of art stops at the 18th century, the time before that is amply covered. In addition to the Renaissance and Baroque paintings, there is an impressive exhibition of Egyptian and Near Eastern statues, sarcophagi and coffins completed by objects of everyday life. The collection of Greek and Roman Antiquities range from the Bronze Age to the early Middle Ages, covering more than three thousand years.

The Kunsthistoriches Museum is a must for anyone who is interested in antique history or fine arts. The many realistic portraits of a royal dynasty will excite you as will the larger than life Egyptian mummy and the enigmatic Brueghel paintings.

For more information, opening hours and ticket prices, or to find out which temporary exhibitions will be visible at the time of your visit, take a look at the official site of the museum at http://www.khm.at/en/

Naturhistoriches Museum (Natural History Museum)

Across the Maria Theresia Square is the counterpart to the Kunsthistoriches Museum: a museum of the same size, with rooms full of treasures of nature. Fossils hiding the secrets of prehistoric times, minerals of great variety, precious stones glittering in myriad of colors, even a huge dinosaur skeleton on display.

The variety of species presented in one place can surprise anyone, and the oldest and most famous statue in the world, the Venus of Willendorf should not be missed (and you might be surprised how small it actually is.) The Naturhistoriches Museum is also a research facility with many exciting findings to show from anthropology to zoology. But the sheer number of mammals, insects and birds on display will make you wonder about the world in which we live. A perfect place to take your children (the tigers and dinosaurs will definitely make an impact upon them.)

To find out more about the collection, the temporary exhibitions, opening hours and prices, visit the official site of the Naturhistoriches Museum at http://www.nhm-wien.ac.at/en?null

Staatsoper (State Opera House)

As the first grand edifice to be finished on the Ringstrasse, the Staatsoper was not only a building, but a statement of power and love for music in the city of Beethoven and Strauss. The Opera House was constructed in a heavily ornate Italian neo-Renassaince architectural style as a tribute to the land and birthplace of opera. The interior is as exquisite as the exterior and when combined with a performance it's a unmissable highlight.

The State Opera has a first-class reputation in the world of music for its eminent performances. It also hosts the first-class Vienna Philharmonic Orchestra, present on the scene for more than 150 years. If you want more than a tour around the empty Opera House, buy a relatively cheap standing ticket for one of its performances. A night at the elegant Staatsoper is an unforgettable experience for anyone who loves classical music.

Österreichische Postsparkasse (Postal Savings Bank)

This building is somehow the odd one out amongst all the major institutions built in the decorative Historicist fashion. It was constructed in the new Viennese style to distinguish it from the pompous Ringstrasse-style. The designer Otto Wagner is famous for his leading role in the Jugendstil (secession) movement which traces its history back to the Postsparkasse headquarters.

The Postal Savings Bank was founded in the 1880s (then in another building) to encourage citizens to save their money and put it in a bank with guaranteed security by the government. This building was constructed at the beginning of the 20th century especially for this purpose. Its steel and concrete, unadorned appearance makes it look safe and impenetrable, creating the feeling in its customers that their money was in good hands.

Innere Stadt (Old Town)

The Innere Stadt is the historical core of the city, and was the whole city itself until 1850, when the demolition of the old city wall started with the construction of the Ringstrasse. It is a beautiful place to visit, full of unexpected treasures to discover. Most of the important landmarks and historical artifacts are located in this area.

Tourist guides often say: "if it's not in the Old Town, it isn't worth seeing". There are, of course, exceptions to this rule, like the Hundertwasserhaus, Schönbrunn Palace and Belvedere Palace, but the fact is that you could spend days just wandering the streets of Innere Stadt and never get bored with the sights it presents.

The best way to explore the Innere Stadt is by walking wherever your feet take you, turning instinctively into a narrow street, stopping in front of an old church or visiting a delicate little boutique. Give yourself time to grasp the small beauties hidden amongst the extravagant palaces, to feel the romantic atmosphere of times gone by.

You will soon find Kärntnerstrasse, the retail heaven of shopaholics, which also hosts (between expensive designer shops) precious antique stores, exclusive restaurants and fine confectioneries like the luxurious Hotel Sacher with its world-famous Sachertorte. This delicatessen costs more than the average Apfelstrudel, but for those who can tell Chocolate Mousse from chocolate cream, its spiritual and palatal value will surely be higher than its price.

Stephansdom (Saint Stephen's Cathedral)

In the center of the Inner Stadt stands one of Vienna's oldest sights, the meeting point in the area, the heart and most important landmark of Austria: the great cathedral called the Stephansdom.

Named after the first Christian martyr, St. Stephen, who was executed for believing in the immortality of Jesus, the cathedral towers over the city protectively. Its earliest parts date to the 13th century, although there had been a religious sight dedicated to the saint on the same spot even before that.

The cathedral was extended over the centuries with the creation of its Gothic facade and tower, the new roof structure and its characteristic colored tiles, the Baroque high altar made of black marble, statues, paintings, reliefs and many priceless historical objects. It is worth taking a guided tour so one can appreciate all the artifacts which have been donated to the church over many generations.

In the Northern tower lies the biggest church bell in Austria weighing more than 20 tons, while the Southern tower was once used by firemen to spot fires around the city. You can climb up the latter, but beware of the 343 steps leading up to it. Although no matter how long the climbing may take, the breathtaking view above the city makes up for your effort.

The Prater

The Prater is one of the oldest amusement parks in Europe. Once a royal hunting ground, in 1766 it was officially donated to public leisure. After that, small cafes, gingerbread stands and merry-go-rounds started to appear to delight the middle-class families of Vienna on a Sunday afternoon, or provide a place to go out on a date for chambermaids or typist girls. In 1873 it hosted the World Exhibition, the only one held in Vienna.

Don't imagine a grand fantasyland the size or diversity of Disneyland in Paris. The Prater is a nostalgic little park with the antique Riesenrad (Giant Ferris Wheel) so memorable in the The Third Man film-noir, haunted castles and ghost trains which only scare the smallest of children, historical roller-coasters more pleasant than exciting. But even adrenaline-junkies will find some rides that make their "hair stand up on the back of their neck", like the Megablitz which turns you over and upside-down in a minute, the Break Dance which shakes you until it almost breaks you, or the Ejection Seat which seems to throw you out in the universe with a speed worthy of a missile.

The Prater can be enjoyed even by visitors who generally don't like amusement parks, as there are more than 250 attractions to choose from. It's ideal to relax here in the summer after a long day's sightseeing.

Secession Building

Around the 1900s, young artists placed it on the map as the center of Jugendstil, (known also by the name Secession, or even more by its French name: Art Nouveau). The art is characterized by flowing lines and geometric curves clearly visible in the city's architecture. The word Jugendstil refers to the style of young architects, sculptors and painters who were opposed to the conservative old artists who were against their attempts to reform art at the turn of the century.

The Secession Building was constructed in 1898, by Otto Wagner's former student, Joseph Olbrich. This gallery was a place where the new association could exhibit the work of its members, and it's still this day the most important Art Nouveau platform in Vienna. Among its most renowned artifacts is the controversial Beethoven Frieze, created by Gustav Klimt and exhibited in the gallery. The pristine white building is crowned by a bronze laurel bush, which was the plant given to Olympic winners and poets in Ancient Greece – the decorators foresaw that one day honor and glory would encircle the members of the Vienna Secession too.

The city is full not only with buildings of the traditional historical styles, but also by modern, Secessionist traces. The Belvedere Palace offers the world's largest Klimt collection, while the metro station (Stadtbahn) entrances at Karlsplatz depict Art Nouveau plants and decorations. Visit the Naschmarkt if you want to see more Wagner-edifices, a delightful place full of life, people and Viennese Secession architecture.

Hundertwasserhaus

The Hundertwasser House in Vienna is one of Austria's most unusual architectural sights. Its curious colorful walls, botanical life, and geometric shapes shows its particular philosophy regarding humans' coexistence with nature.

Its designer thought that a regular city secludes people from their natural habitat. That's why he created the ecological house which lives in harmony not only with its surrounding green environment, but also with its dweller, who can change it according to his or her wishes, to fit his or her personality.

Hundertwasser said that a man has three skins: his own, the clothing he wears and the house he lives in. We have an intimate connection with the first two, so how can we not desire to influence the places we inhabit?

The extravagant building is an eye opener, it makes you think and amazes your senses. Although the Hundertwasserhaus at Kegelgasse can only be admired from the outside since there are tenants living in it, the Kunst Haus Wien is open to everyone.

Have a cup of coffee, or spend some time in the unconventional and not at the least boring Hundertwasser Museum, and you will see how Vienna has more to architecture than the ostentatious Baroque state institutions, and that at any corner you might find something new and inspiring in this city of constant growth and change.

Recommendations for the Budget Traveller

Traveling can be difficult for your bank account balance, no matter how much you try to cut down on your expenses. But there are ways to ensure that you can have the same experience at half the price. No need to bankrupt yourself over accommodation or dining out when there is a great variety of hotels and restaurants ranging from obscenely expensive to "wow, that's less than I expected". Choose from our suggestions below, and you will have the time of your life yet avoid calling this "the most expensive trip of my life."

Places to Stay

Vienna is a tourist-friendly place, so there are many types of accommodations you can consider. Hostels are available for those who want to spend the least amount of money on their bed and breakfast, but there are some clean, spacious hotels which can be booked for very reasonable prices. Try to find out what other guests are saying about the place you fancy booking, and pay attention to its location too: a hotel close to a busy street can save you valuable time and money on transportation, yet the noise arising from the street can probably make you loose sleep if you're sensitive about that.

Here are our suggestions about where to stay in Vienna:

Hotel Ibis Wien Messe

Lassallestrasse 7A, 1020 Vienna, Austria
Tel. (+43)1/217700
Fax. (+43)1/21770556
H2736@accor.com
http://www.accorhotels.com/gb/hotel-2736-ibis-wien-messe/index.shtml
€59 - €92/night

Although not in the Old Town, but still located in the city center and near the Prater. It can be reached by metro (U-Bahn) as well, which also takes you into the Innere Stadt in 5 minute.

The Hotel Ibis Wien Messe offers modern amenities such as air conditioning, daily newspaper, hair dryers, free wireless internet access, television and personal showers. There is also an onsite restaurant to have breakfast for €11. The indoor parking is €10 per day.

Meininger City Hostel & Hotel Vienna

Columbusgasse 16, Vienna, Austria
Tel. 0720 881453
Fax (+43) 1 6032041
welcome@meininger-hotels.com
http://www.meininger-hotels.com/
€29 - €95/night

The Meininger City Hostel & Hotel Vienna is located near St. Stephen's Cathedral, and the Prater and Schönbrunn Palace are close by. It is 2 minutes walk from the Keplerplatz metro station, and about 30 minutes by train from the airport. The hotel is a pet friendly, non-smoking accommodation with mini bar, TV, and shower. It also has a games room complete with PlayStation and available games, billiards table and karaoke machine if you're really set to boogie. The wireless internet is free of charge, so you can send a message home to tell them how great a time you're having.

Hostel Hütteldorf Vienna

Schlossberggasse 8, Vienna, Austria
Tel. (+43) 1 253 0033
Fax (+43) 1 253 0034
hutteldorf@mail.vho.at
http://www.vho.at/hutteldorf/index.en.html
€32 - €111/night

The Hostel Hütteldorf is situated close to the Vienna Forest, so it provides a natural atmosphere to relax after a long day's sightseeing. It is also near many important landmarks, such as the Giant Ferris Wheel at the Prater and St. Stephen's Cathedral, and everything else can be reached by underground. The Vienna International Airport is located within a short distance of the hotel. There are 60 rooms which you can choose from, amongst them several have private baths. Note that every dorm room has lockers. Breakfast is included in the price, but there is no curfew at night, so you can stay as long as you want in the city partying!

Hotel Hadrigan

Maroltingergasse 68, 1160 Vienna, Austria
Tel. (+43) 1 6040000
Fax (+43) 1 6040003
hotel@hadrigan.com
http://www.birghotels.com/en/hotel_hadrigan/
€34 - €99/night

An old-fashioned accommodation, Hotel Hadrigan is a family-run hotel which ensures friendly service and a warm welcome to every guest. Not in a central location, but it's still close to some interesting attractions like the Ottakringer Brauerei, Vienna's last large brewery and Wilhelminenberg Palace. The city center is easily reachable from the hotel, since the tram stop is at the hotel's doorstep and the underground is just 150 meters away for the 15-minute journey into the city center. It has all the amenities one can ask of a hotel, room service, TV, hair dryer, shower, and it also offers a delicious Viennese dinner in the restaurant which is surrounded by a nice little garden.

Palace Hostel Schlossherberge Vienna

Savoyenstrasse 2, Vienna, Austria
Tel. (+43) 1 481 0 300
Fax (+43) 1 481 0 300 13
shb@hostel.at
http://www.hihostels.com/dba/hostels-Vienna---Palace-Hostel-Schlossherberge-004013.en.htm
€45 - €71/night

The Palace Hostel Schlossherberge offers a breathtaking views of Vienna. It is situated on top of a hill, surrounded by forests, meadows and vineyards. Since it's relatively far from the busy city center, it is an ideal place for families who have come to relax and be together in a quiet, beautiful location. Vistors can park for free which is unusual in Vienna. The hotel has free Wi-Fi internet, and you can rent a bike, play volleyball, table tennis or billiards. It is also a "green" hotel, awarded the Austrian eco-label for serving organic products for the breakfast which is included in the price.

Places to Eat

Vienna is as well-known for its cuisine as it is for its landmarks. But you don't need to spend a fortune to eat the famous local dishes as there are plenty of restaurants available for the budget traveler. Or you can grab a bite from the many sausage stands around the city, and try out a Bratwurst sausage, a hot Debreziner or a Käsekrainer enriched with cheese – dine with beer and fresh rolls for a delicious, filling lunch. These are our suggested restaurants to eat at in Vienna:

Figls

Grinzinger 55, Vienna
Tel: (+43) 1 320 42 57
http://www.figls.at/

A more than hundred years old Biergarten with a tavern, the Figls has a great garden and terrace to sit out on a warm summer evening. Prices vary from €7-15, but the historical atmosphere and the excellent traditional Schnitzel is worth every penny.

Esterházykeller

Naglergasse 9, Vienna.
Tel: (+43) 1 5339340
http://www.esterhazykeller.at/

This historic little restaurant offers a great variety of Viennese food at a budget price. Menus and meals start at €6, with lot of meat and home baked deserts and sweets. You can also try out some local wines, directly from the noble Esterházy vineyards and cellars.

Trzesniewski

Dorotheergasse 1, Vienna
Tel: (+43) 1 5123291
http://www.trzesniewski.at/cms2/index.php

Fancy a quick snack before you head back to admire the city? Then this what you're looking for: choose from the dozen types of little sandwiches served with an ice cool beer to freshen you up at only €6.90, right next to Stephansplatz.

Tunnel

Florianigasse 39, Vienna.
Tel: (+43) 1 4053465
http://www.tunnel-vienna-live.at/

A live music venue with a pleasant young vibe and a menu ranging from inexpensive sandwiches, soups, pastas and vegetarian dishes – that's one place worth looking into. Mingle with the locals and listen to live jazz while munching on your food – can this night get any better?

Der Wiener Deewan

Liechtensteinstraße 10, Vienna.
Tel: (+43) 1 925 11 85
http://deewan.at/

Vienna is as multicultural as you would expect from a European metropolis so let's finish our list with a Viennese-Pakistani buffet. The Deewan is based on the concept that you pay more if you enjoy your food, so you can pay as much or as little as you like with no fixed prices and eat all you can. We wish you Guten Appetit.

Places to Shop

Walking around Vienna you will see many boutiques and antique stores. Here are a few places which you should visit to get a flavour of the city.

Naschmarkt

Its name is interconnected which the German "naschen" verb, which means to nibble. And what a place to choose your nibbling from! The market extends for more than 500 m along the Wien river, filled with exotic stands, cafes and beautiful Art Nouveau buildings on Linke Wienzeile street. Fruit, vegetables, fish, meat, pastry, spices and delicatessen - if you can think of it, you will find it here. Step into Scheherazade's Oriental bazaar, and feast your eyes on the diversity of food from around the world.

Flohmarkt

Vienna has a world-famous flea market that is open every Saturday. In the Flohmarkt you can find antiques and bargains for everything: books, clothes, jewelry, furniture, carpets, records, electrics, ornaments etc. It takes a good eye to see beyond the junk to the real value, but the sheer size of this market makes it a cultural event not to be missed.

Leschanz Wiener Schokolade König

Can you think of anything sweeter than chocolate? Nor can we. Chocolatier Leschanz Wolfgang dreamed of creating the world's most beautiful chocolate store. Since its opening in 1844, people dream of having the opportunity to visit it. Handmade chocolate specialties as far as the eye can see in all varieties and shapes. This is a must for everyone with a soft spot for the food of the gods.

Austrian Delights

If you want organic, handmade products, then Austrian Delights is the place to visit. Jams, honey, chutneys, vinegars, wines, cognacs and sweets are all made by local manufacturers and so avoid the impersonal feel of mass-produced food. Even if you don't want to spend a fortune, the free samples make it a trip well worth taking.

Weihnachtsmarkt

Unfortunately these charming places depend on the season, but a treasure-hunter should visit the Viennese Christmas Markets at least once in a lifetime. The atmosphere speaks for itself, but the small stands with colorful merchandise are just as enchanting.

Hand-painted cards, hand-knit scarves, unique blown globes, carved wooden toys - who helped the manufacturers of all of these handmade objects, fairies or dwarfs? Visit Vienna around Christmas and you will have more than a few nice presents to take home with you.

Bratislava

Bratislava on the Danube River has historic palaces, a medieval Old Town, and an interesting set of churches, museums and art galleries. It is the capital and largest city of Slovakia. Located in the southwest of the country, Bratislava is under one hour's drive from Vienna and is the only national capital in the world that borders two other countries (Hungary and Austria).

It occupies both the banks of the popular Danube River and fans out on the left bank of the Morava River.

The city was founded before the 10th century and has been an important seat of power for many kingdoms and states that it has been a part of. Bratislava was a part of the Hungarian kingdom from the 10th century until the World War I. Between the 16th and the mid 19th centuries, Bratislava was the capital and the coronation city of the Kingdom of Hungary. During World War II, it was part of the German-controlled state. Later with the formation of Czechoslovakia it became the capital of the Federal State of Slovakia, until the formation of Slovakia as an independent country in 1993, when it was declared the capital of the independent nation.

The Hungarian influence on the city is evident from the fact that its original name is Hungarian – Pozsony. By the 19th and early 20th century the city was known by its German (or, as some say, Austrian) name Pressburg. The city got its present name Bratislava, as late as 1919.

Due to its importance in the medieval ages, Bratislava has mentions in many other European languages, each in their own form and dialect. However, one that stands out is the Greek name Istrapolis which translates to Danube City, a reference to the famous River Danube which passes through the city and has numerous citations in poems, literary works, and music pieces over the centuries.

Bratislava is a very small city and is often a day-trip for many visitors from the neighboring countries. The historic Old Town is not only the center of the city; it is also the major attraction with all major tourist spots in or around the area.

It can be covered easily in a day. In spite of this small size, Bratislava has been able to attract visitors from central Europe and beyond for its picturesque medieval streets, scenic natural beauty, and over a dozen historic palaces and churches spread all over the city.

Culture

For a city the size of Bratislava, there are ample opportunities for entertainment all the year round. From classical concerts to wild bachelor parties, the city has it all. With its close proximity to Vienna, Bratislava has a strong influence of classical music. It is home to Slovak Philharmonic Orchestra and the Capella Istropolitana – a popular ensemble of chamber music. Birthplace to Johann Hummel and Franz Schmidt, and host to masters like Beethoven, Liszt, and Haydn.

Bratislava has an enviable history of western classical music. Each year, the city hosts the popular Bratislava Music Festival and the Bratislava Jazz Days. The annual Wilsonic Festival attracts crowds and artists from different European countries. Summer times see a lot of the music acts being held at the Bratislava Castle and the parks around Old Town.

Theater lovers can visit the 1000-seat Old Slovak National Theater. Housed in a late 19th century building on the riverfront at the edge of the Old Town, just the visit to the building is an experience in itself. It used to be illuminated with 800 gas lamps.

The interiors are beautifully decorated with frescoes and paintings. A new Slovak National Theater with 1700 seats was opened in 2007 and is also near the Danube waterfront. Both these theaters host opera, ballet and drama. The city has a number of smaller theaters like the Arena Theatre, L+S Theatre, Naïve Theatre, and the Astorka Korzo Theatre.

Bratislava has a number of annual festivals, from cultural to culinary. Popular amongst those are the Bratislava Ball (January), City Marathon (March or April), Easter Market (April), Wine Festival (May), Junifest Beer Festival (June), and the Christmas Market (December). Reenactments of historic Slovak events can be seen at many annual events like the Seize of Bratislava (June), Coronation Celebration (1st weekend every September), and the Festival of Historic Fencing (July & August).

The city is also famous and, at times, infamous for its nightlife. Known to be inexpensive and liberal – highlighted in the popular teen movie Eurotrip in 2004 – the city has attracted many parties from revelers from the city as well as neighboring countries. Popular night clubs in the city include the Loft!, Barrock, Subclub, and the Trafo Music Bar. However, the city is not only about loud wild partying; one can enjoy a drink and local band in many of the pubs and bars in town. Many of these are close to the Old Town. Some of the popular spots include Slovak Pub, Jazz Café, Dubliner Pub, El Diablo Pub, and the Cocoloco Cocktail Bar.

Location & Orientation

The beautiful medieval town of Bratislava is blessed with the proximity to many major Central European cities, making it ideal for 1-2 day trip. It is closest to the Austrian capital, Vienna (about 60 km), making the 2 cities the 2 closest capital cities in Europe. It is about 150 km from Budapest and Graz, and less than 300 km from Zagreb, Prague, Kosice, Warsaw, and Ljubljana. Although the city has a full-fledged working international airport, the close proximity with these neighboring cities and the good condition of the European highways make it ideal to be accessed by road.

The city is served by the Bratislava Milan Rastislav Štefánik Airport (IATA: BTS). The airport is located on the eastern part of the city and is linked through the D1 motorway. With the introduction of low cost carriers, it has been able to draw a considerable number of tourists, especially the younger crowd from the neighboring countries and the UK. The airport is connected to the city through bus and taxi service. Bus no. 61 (to the main railway station in the city), No. 91 (to Petrzalka), and night-bus N61 are available near the Departure terminal. Tickets have to be bought before boarding from the kiosks or manned-counters at the airport. Whereas the bus ticket costs about €1, taxis are much more expensive and could cost up to €30 for a trip to the city center.

For those who are flying in to central Europe can also use the Vienna International Airport (IATA: VIE) – http://www.viennaairport.com/jart/prj3/va/main.jart which is located about 40 km from Bratislava. Regular bus connections (by Postbus and Blaguss) connect the airport with Bratislava. With less than €10 for a ticket, it is a good option for travelers flying in from other continents as there are better and cheaper connections to Vienna.

Bratislava has 2 main train stations – Bratislava hlavn astanica and Bratislava-Petrzalka. Both the stations are well connected by the public bus service. Vienna is just an hour away and is connected by the regional express service twice daily. Prague (4 hrs), Berlin (9 hrs), Budapest (3 hrs), Warsaw (8 hrs), and Belgrade (11 hrs) are connected by the EC train service with multiple daily connections.

With excellent motorways, Bratislava is often accessed by road. In fact, due to the closeness of some of the neighboring major cities, it is actually quicker to take the bus than taking the flight. Major inter-country bus services like Slovak Lines, Eurolines, Orange ways, and Blaguss have multiple connections with Bratislava from not only the neighboring cities, but also from cities as far away as London and Paris. Tickets can be bought at the bus stations or online. It is recommended to buy the tickets in advance, especially for weekend travel and during peak tourist season, as many of these buses get fully booked. Some of the bus services come with in-built toilet, free Wi-Fi, and a beverage counter (against payment) making the travel very comfortable. All long distance buses stop at the Central Terminal (Auto busovastanica) which has trolley-bus and bus connections to different parts of Bratislava.

For those planning to drive, it is necessary to get a vignette (sticker) - to be put on the windshield - once the car enters the Slovakia limits. The vignette can be bought at any gas station. In the city there are 'Park and Walk' facilities. Parking is also available near the city center (the Old Town is auto free zone) but it may be difficult to find a parking space in the narrow one way streets of Bratislava. Kiosks and parking attendants (wearing yellow vests) are available to buy the parking tickets from.

Located on the banks of the Danube, Bratislava is connected by boat services with Vienna. High speed ferry services run daily and cost about €30 for a return ticket.

Once in the city, most of it can easily be covered by foot. Public transport is available through the bus, trolley bus and tram service. Tickets must be bought before boarding and must be validated at the start of the journey. Public transport is also available during the night. A good option for tourists is to buy the Bratislava City Card - http://visit.bratislava.sk/en/vismo/zobraz_dok.asp?id_org=700014&id_ktg=1102&p1=6492.

Climate & When to Visit

Bratislava has a moderately continental climate. It is the sunniest and warmest part of the country with low to moderate rainfall spread all year round. Summer months between April and September have an average high of about 24 degrees Celsius and an average low of about 12 degrees.

Winter months between October and March see an average high of about 7 degrees Celsius and an average low just below freezing. Although the city, especially the Old Town, is beautifully lit up during the Christmas months, it is the summer months that attract most of the tourists to Bratislava for the dry and comfortable weather conditions.

Sightseeing Highlights

Bratislava Castle

Tel: +421 2 544 114 44

Originally built in the 9th century, the Bratislava Castle, perched on a hill on the bank of the River Danube is the most dominating structure on the city skyline. Due to its location on the Little Carpathians rocky hilltop, one can get excellent panoramic views of the city as well as parts of Austria and Hungary from the castle premises. It was declared a National Cultural Monument in 1961 (before the birth of the present day independent country of Slovakia).

Although there are no clear records of the first construction of the castle, it is believed that the castle hill was inhabited from the ancient times. People from the Boleraz culture inhabited there and used a fortified settlement for their protection. Its strategic location made the castle hill an important settlement for the Celts and the Romans until the 5th century AD. About 400 years later – around the 9th century AD during the occupation by the Slavs, a large stone castle was built on the castle hill. Under the Kingdom of Hungary, the city started gaining political and commercial importance and the castle was recognized as one of the major seats of power in the kingdom.

Renovations and expansions went on for the next few centuries with the castle getting a Romanesque as well as Gothic architectural look. During the middle ages it was known as the Pressburg Castle. In the 15th century, there were major rearrangements of the castle and the only surviving part today from the original plan is the Sigismund Gate – popularly known as the Corvinus Gate. Renaissance changes in the early 17th century brought a Baroque look to some parts of the castle. In the 2nd half of the 18th century, the castle was the home to Queen Maria Theresa of the Kingdom of Hungary. Interiors were changed and given a rococo-style finish. Gradients of the stairs were also changed so that the queen could ride her horse through the stairways!

By the early 19th century the castle fell into major disrepair. The 2 world wars saw the castle being used as army barracks. An amphitheater was built in the castle premises. In the mid 1950s a 10-year restoration was done to bring back the glory of the castle.

In the years that followed, the Bratislava Castle was used for many state receptions. A further €50 million was approved in 2008 for restoration of the castle. Although restoration work is ongoing, the castle is open to the public for free and visitors have access to many parts of the castle and the courtyard.

The present castle is a huge rectangular building in white with 4 towers at the 4 corners. The roofs and tower tops are in orange giving the castle a distinct bright look on the green hilltop. There are 4 gates to enter the castle although Leopold Gate is no more accessible. The Sigismund Gate – built in the 15th century – is the oldest gate and is on the southeast of the castle. It is the most used gate for those walking for the Old Town. The Vienna Gate is on the southwest and is accessible through the Palisady Street. This gate is used for those who come by bus or car. The Nicholas Gate on the northwest has the steepest climb through a number of stairs on the hillside. This gate is used by those who come from the Danube riverside.

To the west of the main castle building is the reconstructed 18th century Hillebrandt building. The open space just in front of the castle gates is the Court of Honor. The east of the castle has the 9th century Great Moravian Basilica and the 11th century Church of St Savior. If entering through the Nicholas Gate, one goes through a Gothic gateway that dates back to the 15th century. The Baroque stable at the side of the courtyard has been transformed into a restaurant. The northern border of the castle has an 18th century building that houses the Historical Museum section of the Slovak National Museum.

Grassalkovich Palace

Located in the Hodzovo Square, to the north of the Old Town, is the Presidential Palace or the Grassalkovich Palace. Built in 1760, the palace has a rococo and baroque architectural style and is named after Count Antal Grassalkovich, the head of the Hungarian Chamber for the Kingdom of Hungary. With a French garden on the outside and beautiful rooms, decorated chapel, and a grand staircase on the inside, the palace is one of the most beautiful buildings in the Slovak capital. It is the official residence of the President of Slovakia.

This impressive palace was designed by architect Anton Mayerhofer. The garden at the back of the palace has a statue of Queen Maria Theresa riding a horse. There is also a beautiful Fountain of Youth by noted Slovak sculptor – Tibor Bartfay. Avant-garde statues by various other contemporary sculptors can also be seen in the garden. There is a statue of noted composer Jan Nepomuck Hummel. The garden is open to the public from dawn till sundown. With dogs and bicycles not allowed in the garden, it has become a popular kid's playground. The garden can be accessed through the Banskobrystrická Street and the Stefanikova Street.

The palace was a center for many public gatherings and musical performances in the late 18th century. As Anton was an advisor to Queen Theresa, the palace was used for many royal parties and balls. Joseph Haydn, the legendary composer, was a favorite of Prince Esterhazy, and premiered many of his musicals in this palace.

After the end of World War I, the palace came under the control of the Territorial Military Command. During World War II, it was the seat of the President of the Slovak Republic. After the War, for a few years (1945 to 1950) it was the seat for the ruling Communists. In 1950 the palace was made an activity center for the schoolchildren of Bratislava. The building was extensively damaged by the schoolchildren but renovation was only possible after the end of the Communist rule in 1989. After major reconstructions in the first half of the 1990s, the palace was declared as the official residence of the Slovak President on September 1996.

Michael's Gate

Built sometime around 1300, Michael's Gate is the oldest city gate from the medieval fortifications of Bratislava. It is one of the oldest preserved buildings and stands as one of the gates to the Old Town. It went through major reconstruction in 1758 when it was a given a Baroque look along with a bulbous tower top and a statue of St Michael with the Dragon. Today, standing at 51m, the tower is home to the Weapons Museum section of the Bratislava City Museum.

The entrance to the town (now the Old Town) was heavily fortified in the middle ages. There were 4 heavily fortified gates that controlled the entry and exit. The east of the town had the Laurinc Gate.

To the west was the Fishermen's Gate (as it was mostly used by fishermen who used to bring their catch from the River Danube). To the west was Vydrica Gate or the Black Gate, so named as it was almost in the form of a tunnel. To the north was the Michael's Gate, the only one to have survived the passage of time. It was named after the St Michael's Church that was in front of it. The church was pulled down to finance the extension of the town walls.

In its early years, the gate at St Michael's used to have a drawbridge over a moat for security. A stone bridge later replaced the moat, a structure that stands to date and must be crossed to enter the Old Town through the St Michael's Gate. The gate itself had large wooden doors. For nearly 200 years, newly coronated Hungarian Kings would enter the town through the Vydrica Gate for their coronation and then come to St Michael's Gate to take a pledge of monarchy in the hands of the state's archbishop.

Today, the 7-storey tower houses the Weapons Museum that displays the fortification history of the city. The building, reconstruction, and finally the destruction of the town walls are explained through various exhibits. The 6th floor has a viewing platform from where one can have excellent panoramic views of the Old Town. The street that passes through the St Michel's Gate has a 'zero kilometer plate' and lists the distances of 29 world capitals from that point.

Main Square & Old Town Hall

Certainly one of the most popular tourist spots in the Old Town and home to the Bratislava Christmas Market, the Main Square is located right in the middle of the Old Town. It is dominated by the Old Town Hall and the Roland Fountain that is located on the southwestern corner of the square. Beautiful uniformly colored medieval buildings surround the square. Home to many foreign embassies, these beautiful buildings create a very cheerful ambience to the Old Town center. Cultural programs and concerts are held in the Main Square during the summer months.

The Old Town Hall which stands at the eastern flank of the Main Square is actually a complex of buildings. The buildings and the tower date back to the 14th century, making it one of the oldest stone buildings and the oldest city hall in Slovakia. Three townhouses and a palace were merged to create the present day Town Hall. The buildings that were merged were the Jacobus House (with the tower), the Pawer House, the Unger House, and the Aponyi Palace. The tower, during the early years, used to have a mechanical clock, a sphere showing the phases of the moon, and bells. Today the tower has 4 clock faces and a viewing platform with a 360 degree view of the Old Town. The buildings have gone through several reconstructions and renovations over the years and have a variety of architectural styles – gothic, baroque, neo-renaissance, and neo-gothic. The Town hall is home to the city's oldest museum, the Bratislava City Museum (1868).

The merged buildings were used as the Town Hall until the late 19th century. The buildings also served many other purposes. It was used as a prison, a mint, a municipal archive, and an arsenal depository.

The Weapons Museum in the Town Hall has many interesting exhibits. One of the most popular is a cannonball shot by Napoleon's army in 1809 during their attack on Petrzalka; the cannonball, to this day, is stuck in the tower wall! Other exhibits include medieval torture instruments, armors, weapons, old town dungeons, and some paintings and miniatures. The building, which was originally the Aponyi Palace, is used as a study of Glass and Ceramics.

Old Town Street

A walk though the Old Town of Bratislava is not just a visual treat with the beautiful colored medieval buildings and cobbled streets; it is made interesting and exciting through many quirky statues that have become a major attraction with the visitors.

Rubberneck, or Cumil, is the bronze statue of a man peeking out of a sewerage hole. It is one of the most photographed attractions in the Slovak capital. There is a sign warning oncoming drivers about the statue as it had lost its head twice to reckless drivers. Rubberneck can be seen at the corner of Rybarskabrana, at the junction of Sedlarska and Panska streets.

The Schoner Naci bronze statue is on the Sedlarska Street. This life size statue by Juraj Melus is dedicated to Ignac Lamar, the grandson of a clown who used to walk in the streets of Old Town in the mid 20th century, greeting people and trying to make them smile. Mentally ill but much loved he used to survive on free food given by many of the cafes and restaurants in Old Town. He passed away in 1967; his remains were brought to Bratislava where he was reburied in 2007.

The Paparazzi bronze statue is on Laurinska Street. Dressed in an overcoat and top hat, he is seen aiming his full lens camera from the corner of a building at passers-by.

Located on the Main Square is the bronze statue of Napoleon's Soldier. The statue of this fully uniformed French soldier leans on a bench in the square and provides ample opportunities to be photographed with.

A unique and mischievous stone sculpture can be seen on 29 Panska Street. Located on top of an optician store, it shows a naked man peaking out of a window. There have been many versions to explain the statue; some say he is rushing out so as not to miss the coronation whereas others say that he is mocking a neighbor who used to spy on passersby.

Slavin War Memorial

Commemorating Bratislava's liberation by the Russian Red Army in April 1945, the Slavin War Memorial is a gigantic war memorial that is visible from many parts of the city. Located on a hilltop north of the Bratislava Castle, and standing nearly 50m high, the war memorial is also the cemetery to 6845 Russian soldiers who died in the final weeks of World War II while fighting to free Bratislava and its neighboring regions.

The memorial was designed by Jan Svetlik and opened to the public in 1960 on the 15th anniversary of the liberation of the city. It was declared a National Cultural Monument a year later. The impressive memorial has a central obelisk which rises 39m; this is topped by the statue of a victorious soldier carrying the Soviet flag, which rises another 11m in height. There is a bronze door that opens into the memorial auditorium. The central solemn hall has a number of statues and inscriptions; there is also a white marble sarcophagus. The base of the memorial has the inscriptions of the names of the Slovak cities that were liberated by the Russian Red Army during their westward advance in the last 2 years of the World War II.

The memorial symbolizes the gratitude the Slovaks had towards the Russians for liberating them from the German Wehrmacht units. However, the relations soured considerably when the Soviet backed Communist Party ousted Alexander Dubcek, the popular Slovak leader, and gained control of Czechoslovakia in the late 1940s.

Today, the war memorial, located in one of the wealthier districts of Bratislava with foreign embassies and rich residences, is a great place for a relaxed stroll. The panoramic views of the city from the memorial are spectacular making the memorial a must-visit place, especially on a clear sunny day.

Novy Most (New Bridge)

The Most Slovenskéhonárodnéhopovstania (which translates to Bridge of the Slovak National Uprising or Most SNP), commonly known as the Novy Most or New Bridge is on the River Danube connecting the southern part of the Old Town to Petrzalka on the south bank of Bratislava. The bridge was originally named Most SNP in 1972; the name was changed to New Bridge in 1993, and then changed back to Most SNP on August 2012.

Completed in 1972, after a 5-year construction, the bridge ranks 32nd in the World Federation of Great Towers; making it the shortest tower as well as the only bridge in the rankings. The Most SNP is the longest cable stayed bridge in the world which has a single pylon and one cable-stayed plane. The Most SNP stretches 430.8 m (the main span on the water is 303 m) in length and has a steel construction that is suspended from steel cables.

The Most SNP is easily identifiable by the 84.6 m pylon near the Petrzalka end of the bridge; on top of the pylon is a flying saucer-shaped restaurant.

Originally called the Bystrica, it was renamed UFO in 2005 prompting many people to call the Most SNP, the UFO Bridge. The east pillar of the pylon has an elevator reaching up to the restaurant that has excellent views of the River Danube and both banks of the Slovak capital. The west pillar has a 430-step staircase for emergency evacuation. The bridge itself has 2 levels, the upper level is open to motor traffic and has 4 lanes, and the lower level is for bicycles and pedestrians.

St Martin's Cathedral

One of the most common photographs of Bratislava is from the Bratislava Castle hilltop overlooking the Old Town skyline. The most dominating tower (spire) of the skyline is that of the St Martin's Cathedral, a 15th century Catholic cathedral. Affiliated to the Roman Catholic Archdiocese of Bratislava, it is the largest and one of the oldest churches in the city. It is of great historical importance. Located on the southwestern boundary of the Old Town, the church was a part of the medieval fortifications. It was also the coronation church to the Kingdom of Hungary. Between 1563 and 1860, the coronation parade would enter through the Black Gate on the west wall, go to the St Martin's Cathedral for the coronation, and then head to the St Michael's Gate for the oath to the state's archbishop.

The cathedral with its 85 m tall spire is built in a classic crucifix shape. The top of the spire has a 300-kg gilded replica of the Hungarian Royal crown.

The nave of the cathedral has 3 aisles. It is built amidst a spacious courtyard with cobblestoned side-streets. Beautiful stained-glass windows adorn the interior.

The original church was in the neighboring Bratislava Castle but had to be shifted out in the 13th century for security reasons to the spot where the present cathedral is. Originally a Romanesque church was built but was replaced by a bigger and new Gothic cathedral that was commissioned in the early 14th century. Construction was completed in the mid 15th century – in 1452. The church and the spire had gone through numerous renovations and reconstructions over the centuries due to many disasters – fire, lightning, earthquake, as well as war. Parts of the St Martin's Cathedral were restructured to build the Most SNP which has its northern end in front of the cathedral.

Primate's Palace

Located in the Old Town is the impressive late 18th century neo-classical building, the Primate's Palace. Originally built for the Archbishop, it is today the seat of the Bratislava Mayor. The palace has a north facing façade built in a classical style of architecture. The roof has a number of allegorical statues depicting the different human qualities and achievements. On the top of the tympanum is the coat of arms of the first occupant of the palace – Cardinal Jozef Batthyanyi. A 150-kg iron model of the cardinal's hat crowns the top of the palace.

One of the most popular halls in the palace is the Hall of Mirrors. The early 19th century Treaty of Bratislava between Austria and France was signed in the Hall of Mirrors. Nowadays, the hall is used to host concerts. The city purchased the Primate's Palace in 1903 and during a reconstruction the same year, rare 17th century English tapestry produced in the English town of Mortlake was discovered inside the palace. The Hall of Mirrors and the tapestry are open for public viewing making the palace worth a visit when in Bratislava.

Slovak National Museum

Tel: +421 2 204 69 114
http://www.snm.sk/?home

Established in 1961, the Slovak National Museum is a combination of 18 national museums, 8 of which are located in the capital city, Bratislava. Headquartered in Bratislava, the museum has a total collection of 3894000 objects, which amounts to nearly 40% of the total museum collections in Slovakia. It is the primary institution in Slovakia that is focused on the cultural education and research in museological activity in the country. From ancient every day tools to fancy facilities used by the nobles in the Middle Ages, the different museums have a variety of collections that could interest people from different backgrounds.

The museums located in the city include the Natural Science Museum, Archeological Museum, Museum of History, Music Museum, Museum of Jewish Culture, Museum of Hungarian Culture in Slovakia, Museum of Carpathian German Culture, and the Museum of Croatian Culture in Slovakia.

Recommendations for a Budget Traveller

Places to Stay

Falkensteiner Hotel Bratislava

Pilarikova 5
Bratislava
Tel: +421 2 592 36 100
http://www.falkensteiner.com/en/hotel/bratislava

The Falkensteiner Hotel Bratislava is a 4 star property that is located to the west of the Old Town, near the St Michael's Gate. This stylish modern hotel has a 24 hr reception, VIP room service, and a concierge service. Airport transfers and parking can be arranged by the hotel. There is an onsite restaurant, bar, executive lounge, and snack vending machines. Pets are allowed. There is free Wi-Fi. Rooms are very spacious and equipped with all modern facilities with rates starting from €139.

Hotel SET

Kaliniciakova 29
Nove Mesto, Bratislava
Tel: +421 2 491 09 600
http://en.hotelset.sk/

Located in the Nove Mesto district, Hotel SET is a 4 star property with the National Tennis Center and the hockey stadium in close proximity. This non-smoking property has free Wi-Fi and parking. There is a 24 hr reception. Pets are allowed. There is an onsite restaurant, bar, and ATM machine. Rooms are ensuite and with all modern facilities. Rates start from €48 including breakfast.

Hotel Matsyak

Prazska 15
Bratislava
Tel: +421 2 206 3 4001
http://www.hotelmatysak.sk/home/

This 3 star hotel is located right across the road from the main train station. The closest major attraction is the Slavin War Memorial. There is free parking and a 24 hr front desk. Facilities include onsite restaurant, bar, and currency exchange. There is free LAN internet in the rooms. The specialty of the hotel is the elaborate wine cellar with more than 40000 bottles! Rooms are elegantly decorated with rates starting from €70.

Hotel Abba

Stefanikova 4
Bratislava
Tel: +421 2 5751 1000
http://www.abbabratislavahotel.com/en

Located close to the Slavin War Memorial and the Grassalkovich Palace, the Hotel Abba is a new hotel with modern rooms and excellent facilities which include a 24 hr reception, free Wi-Fi, onsite restaurant, snack bar, bicycle rental, and a travel desk. All the 125 rooms are equipped with the latest convenience with prices starting at €60.

Austria Trend Hotel

Vysoka 2A
Bratislava
Tel: +421 2 52 775 800
http://www.austria-trend.at/hotel-bratislava/en/

This 4 star hotel is located very close to the Grassalkovich Palace. It has 24 hr front desk, VIP room service, and a concierge service. Pets are allowed. There is free Wi-Fi. There is an onsite restaurant and a bar. It also has a sauna and a fitness center. All the 199 rooms are ensuite and have 'every conceivable comfort'. Room rates start from €80.

Places to Eat

UFO

Novy Most (Most SNP)
Bratislava
Tel: +421 2 62 52 0300
http://www.redmonkeygroup.com/

Located on the Most SNP (bridge) on the River Danube, this is one of the most impressive restaurant addresses in Bratislava. The 2-page menu includes a 7-course dinner (€75) and a 3-course lunch (€30). The restaurant also serves a wide variety of wine and spirits. There is a bar located 85m above ground level having excellent panoramic views of the city. The entry fee (€6.50) for the 95m high viewing level is waived for the restaurant guests.

Slovak Pub

Obchodna 62
Bratislava
Tel: +421 2 5263 3285
http://www.slovakpub.sk/

The Slovak Pub is not just a pub but also a full-fledged restaurant, and certainly one of the best places to try authentic Slovak cuisine.

The place has a medieval pub décor with some of the interior pieces dating back nearly 200 years! Main dishes are priced around €5 making it very pocket friendly too, one of the reasons why it may be very crowded in the evenings. The Slovak Pub is located just outside the Old Town.

Altitude Restaurant

Cestana Kamzik 14
Bratislava
Tel: +421 2 4425 69 46
http://www.altitude.sk/?blogs=altitude_uvod&lang=en

Aptly named, this is the highest restaurant in Bratislava and has a 360 degree view of the city. It is located in the 195m high Kamzik TV Tower. Altitude has a brasserie, a restaurant, a passage bar, and a dance hall. European and Slovak cuisine is served with the main dishes priced between €12 & €26. Desserts are priced about €6. Excellent cuisine, great views, and an elegant atmosphere make the visit to the Altitude a great experience.

Antica Toscana

Madarska 27
Bratislava
Tel: +421 2 6285 9307
http://www.anticatoscana.sk/

Open every day except Monday, this is one of the finest Italian restaurants in Bratislava.

It has both indoor and outdoor seating. Waiters are prompt and helpful. It has a big variety of authentic Italian pastas (and risottos) which is specially recommended. This small cozy restaurant uses original Italian spices for the preparation. A full meal costs between €5 and €10.

Hradna Hviezda

Bratislava Castle
Tel: 0944 14 27 18
http://www.hradnahviezda.sk/

This elegantly decorated restaurant is part of the Bratislava Castle. Although the prices are on the higher side, the delicious food and excellent service makes it worth it. It serves various European cuisines like Slovak, English, French, Italian, and German. The prices for the main dishes range between €15 and €20. It also serves wine from the neighboring Carpathian vineyards.

Places to Shop

Old Town Christmas Market

A must-visit market if one is visiting Bratislava in December, the Christmas Market is concentrated at the courtyard in front of the Old Town Hall.

Concerts and light shows keep the place lively every evening. It is the ideal place to not only buy some traditional Slovak gifts but also to try the local mulled wine and potato pancakes.

Aupark Shopping Center

Located in Einsteinova, this modern shopping center has all the convenience and offerings of a modern mall. There is a grocery super market, cinema complex, fitness center, and over 25 different eateries and pubs. There is also a car wash and a children's play area.

Polus City Center

This huge shopping center is located in the Nove Mesto district of the city. It has a shopping center, hypermarket, fitness center, cinema complex, and a post office in its premises. There is also a casino arcade that is open 24 hrs. There are over two dozen places to eat or drink, from fine dining to fast food.

Old Town

The auto free zone inside the Old Town is the ideal place to not only have a stroll on the medieval streets but also to buy varieties of products – from branded items like Gucci and D&G to hand-made crafts of Slovakia. The streets also have many souvenir stores selling a wide variety of products aimed at tourists.

Obchodna Street

Obchodna is one of the most happening streets with plenty of bars and boutique stores. The street leads right up to the St Michael's Gate of the Old Town. On one side of the street there are a number of hostels and budget accommodations. On the other side of the street, along with plenty of restaurants, bars, and ice cream parlors, one can find stores on fashion and accessories. A small lane off the Obchodna leads into a street market where one can buy winter clothes at a bargain.

Printed in Great Britain
by Amazon.co.uk, Ltd.,
Marston Gate.